Jet, the pet, lived in a hutch next to the shed.

He was sad.

He had no fresh green grass.

One day Jet got out of the hutch. He went to look for some fresh green grass.

Jelly and Bean went to look for Jet.

"I will catch him," said Jelly.

"I will catch him," said Bean.

Jelly went to look in the hut.

She did not catch Jet.

Bean went to look in the shed.

He did not catch Jet.

Jelly went to look in the mud next to the log.

She did not catch Jet.

Bean went to look in the bushes.

He did not catch Jet.

Then they saw Jet in a ditch.

"I will catch him," said Jelly.

"I will catch him," said Bean.

Jet did not run away.

He had cut his leg.

Jelly and Bean had to help him out of the ditch.

They took Jet back to his hutch.

Then they put lots of fresh green grass in it.

Jet was happy now.